Queen Elizabeth
Islands

Severnaya
Zemlya

Franz
Joseph Land

Baffin Bay

Svalbard

Barents Sea

Greenland

Greenland
Sea

words & pictures

# CONTENTS

# WHAT IS THE ARCTIC?

The Arctic is the northernmost part of our planet. At its heart is the frozen Arctic Ocean, along with icy cold seas and bays. Surrounding the ocean are the northern lands of Alaska, Canada, Russia, Norway, Sweden, and Finland, as well as large islands, such as Greenland and Iceland.

## Two North Poles

Did you know our planet has two North Poles? The Earth constantly spins around an imaginary line, like a spinning top. The northern point of this line is the "geographic North Pole" (the Pole we refer to in this book). However, because the Earth wobbles, this pole is not always in the same place —it moves about 4 inches (10 cm) a year! Nearby is the second North Pole—called the "magnetic North Pole." This is at the northern end of the Earth's magnetic field (an invisible area of force that surrounds our planet). A compass needle points toward the magnetic North Pole, but this pole moves too! When the Earth's magnetic field changes, the magnetic pole shifts its position.

Magnetic North Pole

Geographic North Pole

Geographic South Pole

Magnetic South Pole

## Ice on the move

The sea ice in the Arctic Ocean moves around constantly. Driven by the wind, a large part of the ice drifts slowly clockwise around the North Pole. Recently, scientists have noticed that the ice is moving faster. This is likely to be caused by global warming and climate change, which are also making the ice melt. Lots of melting ice will cause sea levels to rise, which is bad news for our planet.

## Iceberg ahead!

Many places in the north of our planet have glaciers. These "rivers of ice" flow downhill until they reach the sea. Here, the glacier breaks up into icebergs, in a process known as "calving." Floating in the sea, with only a small part showing above the surface, the icebergs drift slowly southward into warmer waters, and melt. The iceberg that was famously struck by the *Titanic* in the North Atlantic Ocean probably came from a glacier in Greenland.

Sled dogs, such as huskies, are capable of pulling sleds at 10-16 miles (16-26 km) per hour.

## A PLACE OF EXTREMES

One of the coldest towns on Earth is Verkhoyansk in Arctic Russia. In the winter, the temperature once dropped to minus 90 degrees Fahrenheit (-68°C). However, one summer, it soared to 99 degrees Fahrenheit (37°C)! The people who live in Verkhoyansk encounter the greatest range of temperature experienced anywhere in the world.

## An icy desert

At the North Pole, the winter air temperature averages minus 40 degrees Fahrenheit (-40°C). In summer it is common to reach 32 degrees Fahrenheit (0°C). In winter, the Pole is slightly warmer than the rest of the Arctic mainland, because warm water from the south flows into the Arctic Ocean. Despite its cold temperatures, the Arctic is a polar desert, as little rain or snow falls, even in winter. The average total is only 13.6 inches (345 mm) of rain each year.

## Lights in the sky

On clear nights in the Arctic, the sky is sometimes lit up with dancing curtains of green, purple, and pink light. This is the aurora borealis, or Northern Lights. It occurs because the Sun sends out tiny particles into space. The particles react with gases in the Earth's upper atmosphere above the North Pole. The result is a breathtaking winter light show.

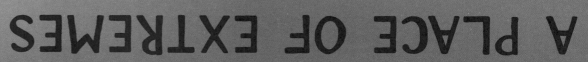

# Woolly coats for winter

To keep warm during the Arctic winter the musk ox has two thick coats: an outer layer of long hairs and an inner layer of soft wool. The soft under wool is shed in spring and people from northern lands collect it. Called qiviut, it is considered to be eight times cozier than sheep's wool, making it one of most valuable natural fibers on Earth.

Faced with a wolf pack, musk oxen bunch closely together with their horns facing outward.

# Snowy camouflage

The main enemy of the musk ox is the Arctic wolf. The wolf has a thick layer of body fat and a snug winter coat to keep its body warm. Its small ears reduce heat loss. The wolf has fur on its paws, which keeps them warm and provides better grip in icy conditions. The Arctic wolf's fur is white or gray, which helps it to blend in with its snowy background and creep up on its prey without being spotted.

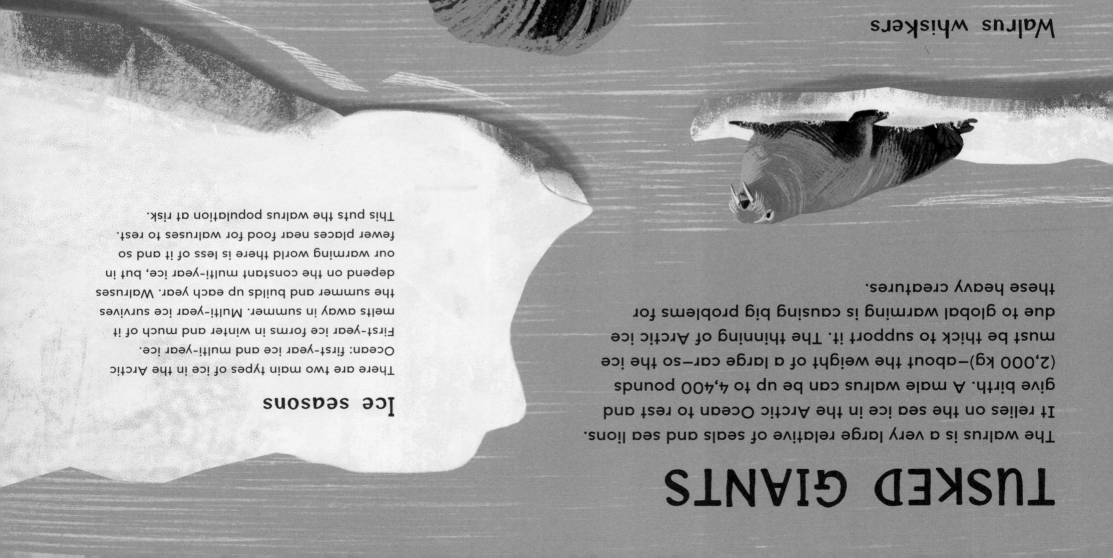

# TUSKED GIANTS

The walrus is a very large relative of seals and sea lions. It relies on the sea ice in the Arctic Ocean to rest and give birth. A male walrus can be up to 4,400 pounds (2,000 kg)—about the weight of a large car—so the ice must be thick to support it. The thinning of Arctic ice due to global warming is causing big problems for these heavy creatures.

## Ice seasons

There are two main types of ice in the Arctic Ocean: first-year ice and multi-year ice. First-year ice forms in winter and much of it melts away in summer. Multi-year ice survives the summer and builds up each year. Walruses depend on the constant multi-year ice, but in our warming world there is less of it and so fewer places near food for walruses to rest. This puts the walrus population at risk.

## Walrus whiskers

Adult walruses have long tusks and coarse whiskers. They dive down to the seabed and use their sensitive whiskers to find clams. They blow jets of water at the clams to clear away the mud, then clamp their mouth around the shellfish and suck out the soft parts.

## Warm as a walrus

Under its thick, wrinkled skin a walrus has a layer of blubber that keeps it warm in the cold Arctic Ocean. Another feature which keeps a walrus warm is its blood vessels. In the icy water, their blood vessels in their skin shrink to reduce heat loss, so walruses can appear paler in color. When a walrus hauls out onto beaches in summer, it warms up, so the opposite happens—the blood vessels open up, blood flows to the skin, and the walrus turns pink!

# ARCTIC SEALS

There are six types of seal living in the Arctic, all generally found at the edge of the ice pack. Most seals give birth on the ice, and have special ways to help their pups avoid predators, such as polar bears.

## Hooded seal

The male hooded seal has an interesting habit during breeding season: it blows up its nose like a balloon! Other males are threatened by this, while females find it attractive. A mother hooded seal gives birth on top of the sea ice, but the baby does not stay there for long. A mother produces about 5.8 gallons (22 liters) of thick milk per day, which is so rich (more like runny butter than milk) that the pup grows very quickly. In just four days, it doubles in size and is ready to live on its own—the shortest suckling time of any mammal. This quick growth reduces a pup's chance of being attacked by a polar bear on the ice, and is very important for its survival.

The male hooded seal can inflate the gray hood on his snout and also the pinky-red membrane between his nostrils.

## Harp seal

A mother harp seal suckles her white-coated pup for just 12 days and then leaves it on the top of the ice. After a few days alone, the pup sheds its white coat and grows a gray one. It then teaches itself to swim and starts to hunt fish at just four weeks old.

## Spotted seal

These seals live alone for part of the year but gather together in large groups at breeding time. Pups have a white coat at first, and they are suckled for two to four weeks.

## Ribbon seal

This seal has white bands on its dark body. Pups are born on thin ice, which reduces the risk of heavy polar bears approaching. Youngsters are white at first, and are nursed for four to six weeks. Their mothers teach them how to dive for food.

## Bearded seal

This seal has a distinctive mustache of long, thick bristles. At breeding time, males make elaborate sounds underwater in order to attract females and scare away other males. Pups are born on the ice and are ready to leave their mothers after 18 to 24 days.

# SNOW DEN ATTACK

## A giant among bears

The polar bear competes with the Kodiak brown bear for the title of the world's largest bear. A male polar bear can be up to 10 feet (3 m) long and keeps warm with a thick layer of fat and two layers of fur. The bears look white, but in fact their skin is black and their hairs are hollow and transparent. They appear white because of the way the sunlight bounces off their hair.

The sixth type of Arctic seal is the ringed seal. This is the smallest and most common seal in the Arctic. Seal pups are often born in snow lairs or dens on the ice, built by their mothers to keep them safe. Despite its building efforts, ringed seals are so common and widespread that they are the main prey of the polar bear, which will attack the seals inside their snowy lairs.

## Ultimate Arctic hunters

Polar bears have an amazing sense of smell, and are able to detect a ringed seal on the ice from about 0.6 mile (1 km) away, or inside a snow lair under three feet (about 1 m) of snow. If it smells a seal in its lair, the bear will crash into the den and grab the pup. A bear will also wait at a breathing hole for a ringed seal to pop up, and then grab it with its powerful forepaws.

## Ringed seal lair

The mother ringed seal enters the lair via a hole in the ice below, which leads into the water. The large claws on her front flippers are used to keep open breathing holes in the ice. It is the only northern seal that does this. Each mother builds several lairs, so she and her pup have somewhere safe to go if predators try to break in.

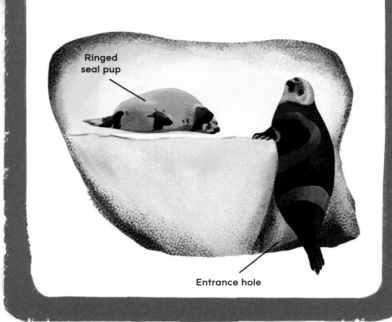

Ringed seal pup

Entrance hole

## Canine companion

Arctic foxes follow polar bears in order to steal some of their food. They sometimes travel long distances over the ice. One fox was followed by scientists for 2,179 miles (3,506 km) from Spitsbergen, across the Arctic Ocean ice pack, to Greenland. Even then it did not stop and continued on to Ellesmere Island in the Canadian Arctic.

# POLAR BEAR IS KING

Polar bears depend on the Arctic sea ice for hunting, so when it breaks up in summer they have a problem. With more open water, the seals have the advantage and can swim quickly away. Some polar bears leave the Arctic Ocean and its melting ice floes in summer, and head for the coast. Here, they feed on all sorts of unexpected foods, from berries and seaweed, to birds' eggs and chicks. The more resourceful bears, however, have their sights set on much larger items of food…

## Scavenging bears

Polar bears sometimes scavenge on the carcasses of whales that have been killed by local people or have died naturally. They can pick up the smell of rotting meat from many miles away.

Beluga whale

## Patient hunters

In the estuary of the Seal River, which flows into Canada's Hudson Bay, polar bears perch on isolated rocks in the sea and wait patiently for the tide to rise. Belugas or white whales arrive with the incoming tide. If a whale gets close to the rock, the bear leaps onto its back, kills it, and hauls it to the shore to eat. It's quite a challenge, as a beluga is three times heavier than a bear, and more agile in the water. Successful bears are among the best fed in the Arctic. While other bears lose weight in summer, these bears put it on!

# Walrus panic

Walruses "haul out," or gather, on beaches in huge numbers during the summer.
These colonies are a magnet for polar bears. The adult walruses are generally too
big to kill, and they have long tusks to jab at any bear that comes too close, so instead,
the bears look for walrus pups. They rush at the colony, panic the adults, and try to seize
youngsters while their mothers are distracted.

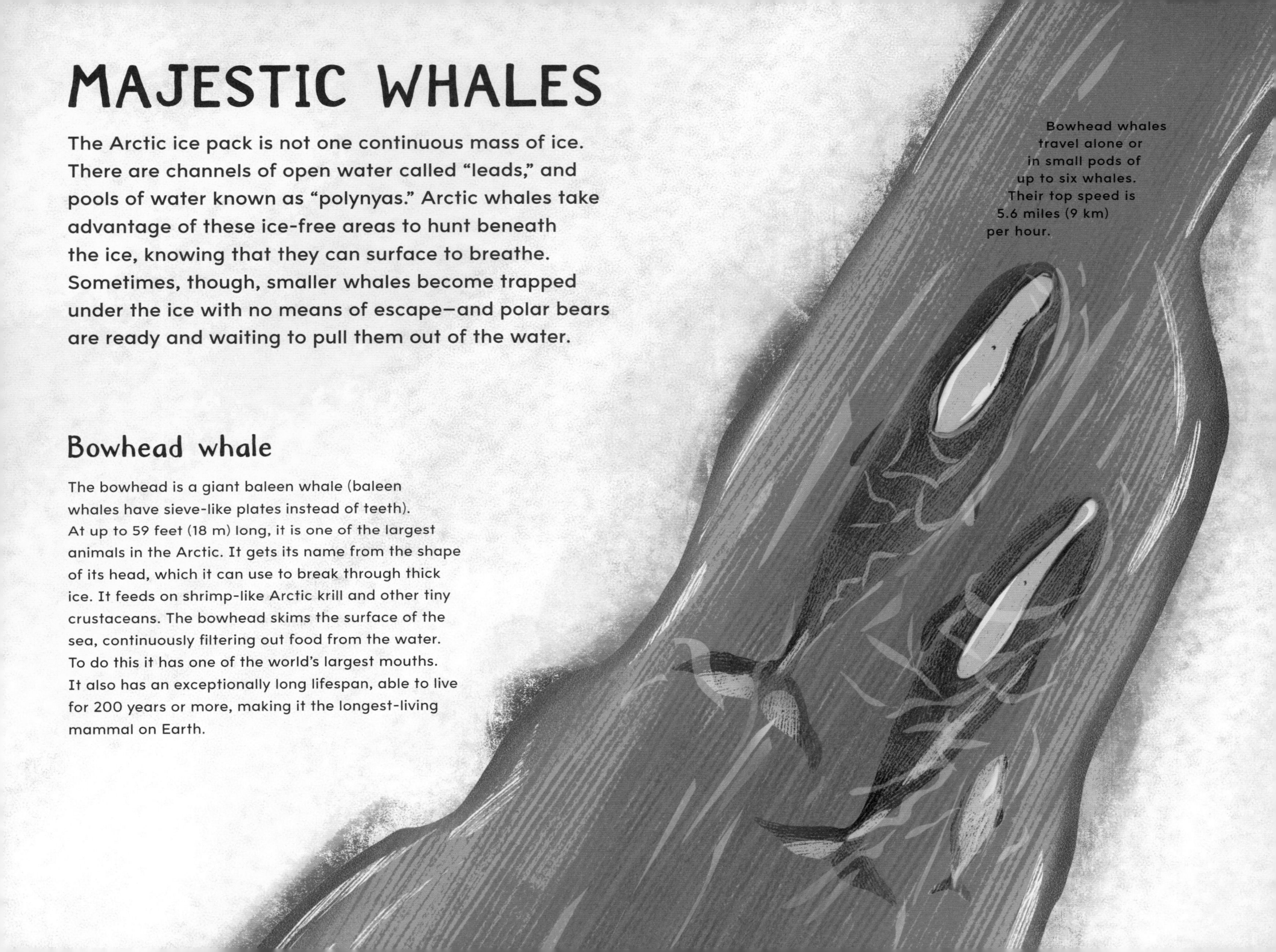

# MAJESTIC WHALES

The Arctic ice pack is not one continuous mass of ice. There are channels of open water called "leads," and pools of water known as "polynyas." Arctic whales take advantage of these ice-free areas to hunt beneath the ice, knowing that they can surface to breathe. Sometimes, though, smaller whales become trapped under the ice with no means of escape—and polar bears are ready and waiting to pull them out of the water.

Bowhead whales travel alone or in small pods of up to six whales. Their top speed is 5.6 miles (9 km) per hour.

## Bowhead whale

The bowhead is a giant baleen whale (baleen whales have sieve-like plates instead of teeth). At up to 59 feet (18 m) long, it is one of the largest animals in the Arctic. It gets its name from the shape of its head, which it can use to break through thick ice. It feeds on shrimp-like Arctic krill and other tiny crustaceans. The bowhead skims the surface of the sea, continuously filtering out food from the water. To do this it has one of the world's largest mouths. It also has an exceptionally long lifespan, able to live for 200 years or more, making it the longest-living mammal on Earth.

## Beluga

The beluga or white whale is a small whale with teeth instead of baleen plates. It is about 18 feet (5.5 m) long, and is adapted to an Arctic lifestyle in several ways. It is pure white, and it has no dorsal (back) fin, which enables the whale to swim under the ice without any fin getting caught. It has a rounded forehead—known as the melon—that is part of the beluga's guidance system. It finds its way in the gloom below the ice using sound; in fact, the beluga whale is known as the "sea canary" because of the variety of sounds it makes.

## Narwhal

Narwhals are also toothed whales, and are about the same length as belugas. Male narwhals have a long, spiral tusk growing out of their upper jaw, which can be up to 10 feet (3 m) long. It's not clear why the narwhals have a tusk, but they have been seen to use it to slash at shoals of Arctic cod during feeding. The tusk also has many nerve endings, so scientists think it could be used to check the condition of the water. This does not explain, however, why most female narwhals do not have tusks. It seems to be a male thing, which suggests it is also used for attracting a mate.

# LIFE UNDER THE ICE

We know very little about life under the Arctic ice, because it is dangerous and very difficult to reach. Modern submarines with video cameras and special nets that can catch creatures beneath the ice are revealing a wealth of marine life in the ice-cold waters. Skeleton shrimps, sea butterflies, sea angels, brittle stars, deep-sea snailfish, and many, many more creatures have been discovered.

Psychedelic jellyfish

## Arctic cod

The most common fish in the Arctic Ocean is the Arctic cod. Seabirds, seals, and whales all depend on it. The fish can survive in the ice-cold water because it has antifreeze in its blood. Young cod hide in the labyrinth of cracks, caves, and dimples on the underside of the ice. Here, they feed on tiny animals, such as copepod crustaceans. It's a bit like the sea floor, but upside down!

## The food chain

At the bottom of the Arctic Ocean food chain is the phytoplankton or "plant-like plankton"—mainly different types of algae and bacteria—that float close to the surface or under the ice. Like plants on land, these tiny living things use sunlight to produce their own food. In spring, there is increasingly more light and the ice melt releases more nutrients, so the phytoplankton blooms. All life in the Arctic Ocean benefits from the sudden bonanza of food.

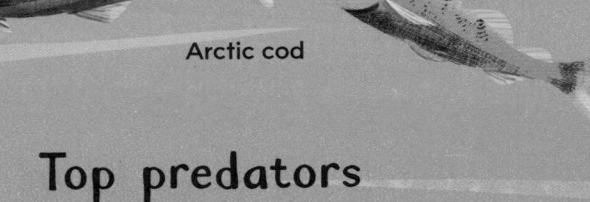
Arctic cod

Northern sea nettle jellyfish

## Top predators

Phytoplankton is eaten by small animals, such as krill. Then jellyfish, sea anemones, small squid, and fish catch the krill. Those bigger animals become the prey of even larger fish. They, in turn, are food for seals and small whales, which are hunted by killer whales and polar bears—referred to as "apex predators" because they are at the top of the food chain.

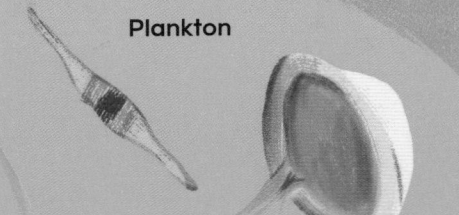
Plankton

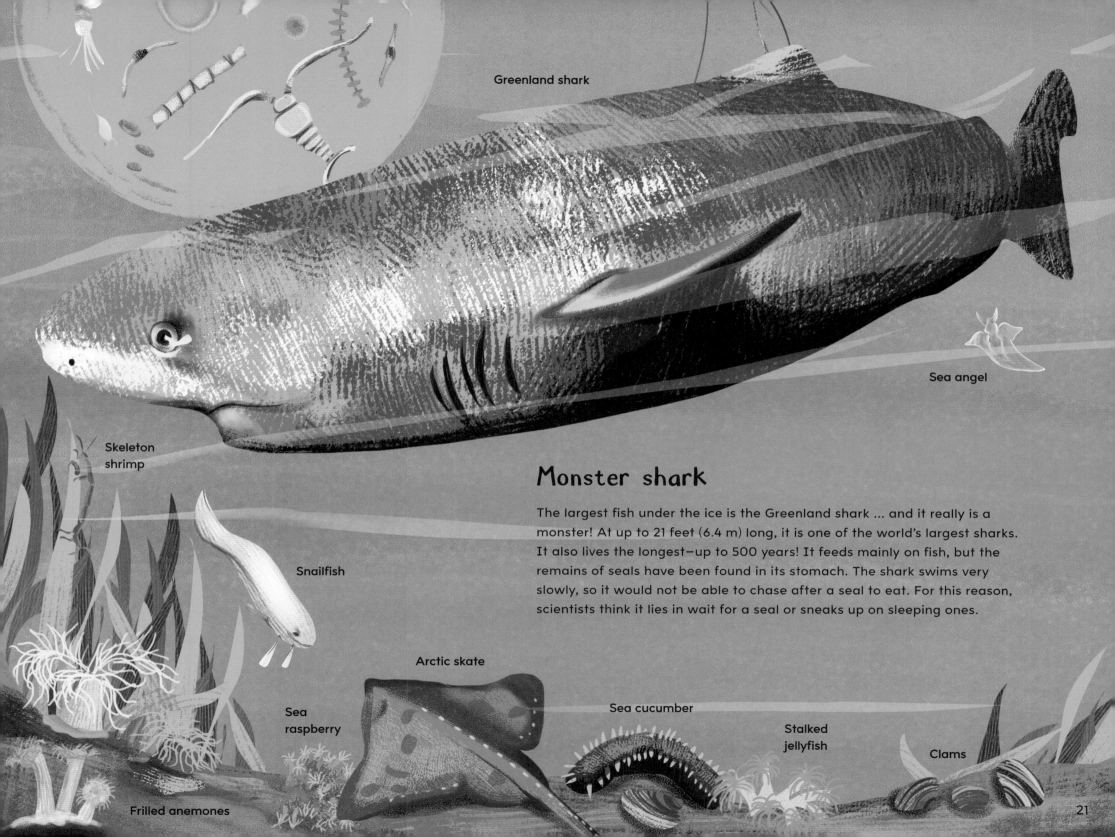

Greenland shark

Sea angel

Skeleton shrimp

## Monster shark

The largest fish under the ice is the Greenland shark ... and it really is a monster! At up to 21 feet (6.4 m) long, it is one of the world's largest sharks. It also lives the longest—up to 500 years! It feeds mainly on fish, but the remains of seals have been found in its stomach. The shark swims very slowly, so it would not be able to chase after a seal to eat. For this reason, scientists think it lies in wait for a seal or sneaks up on sleeping ones.

Snailfish

Arctic skate

Sea cucumber

Sea raspberry

Stalked jellyfish

Clams

Frilled anemones

# SEABIRD CITIES

All around the Arctic in summer, high sea cliffs are packed with millions of nesting seabirds. They arrange themselves so that different species are at different heights on the cliff. Little auks are found among the loose rocks at the bottom and guillemots lay their eggs on narrow ledges closest to the sea. Fulmars and kittiwakes nest on ledges higher up, while puffins dig burrows at the top.

## Cliffside predators

The smell and noise from seabird colonies is extraordinary, so they attract a lot of predators. Glaucous gulls steal guillemot eggs, and white-tailed eagles target kittiwake chicks. Like pirates, Arctic skuas harass seabirds returning to the nest and rob them of their hard-won catch.

Puffins

Arctic skua

Kittiwakes

Fulmars

## Little auks and puffins

The little auk, or dovekie, is the only Atlantic auk to have a throat pouch, which it uses to collect food to bring back to its young. The bird dives underwater to catch krill and small fish. It then stores them in its throat pouch, like a hamster, and flies back to the nest. The puffin adopts a different technique. It catches sand eels and other small fish, and carries several of them crossways in its bill like a "fish mustache" as it flies back to the nest.

# Fulmars

Fulmars look like gulls but they are more like albatrosses, and fly on stiff wings. They also have a rather disgusting way of defending themselves from predators or rivals: they bring up foul-smelling stomach oil and spray it at an attacker. It clogs the plumage of any bird predator that comes too close, stopping them from flying.

# Guillemot chicks

The guillemot, or murre, is a black-and-white seabird that looks a bit like a penguin. At the end of the breeding season, guillemot chicks do the most amazing thing: they launch themselves off the cliff before they have even learned to fly! Encouraged by their parents, they try to glide toward the sea. Some fall short and bounce onto the rocks, where they are in danger of being gobbled up by Arctic foxes. The successful ones spend the next few months out at sea with their fathers learning to fly and to dive for food.

Guillemots

Glaucous gull

Little auks

Arctic fox

Guillemots

# ARCTIC TUNDRA

Tundra is the name given to the lands surrounding the Arctic Ocean. The soil below the tundra is permanently frozen, so it is called "permafrost." There are few plants, and almost no trees. Even so, there are many different animals living here, and their numbers swell enormously in summer as migrating birds arrive to breed.

## Flight of the snow goose

Snow geese arrive in the Arctic during summer to nest in remote spots where they are safe from most predators. Only Arctic foxes and skuas dare to face an angry mother goose. Snow geese sometimes migrate in such large numbers that the flock looks like a snowstorm.

## Arctic wanderers

Both male and female reindeer (caribou) have antlers, which they use in winter to dig beneath the snow to find plants to eat. They have large spreading hooves that enable them to walk over snow or soggy ground. Some reindeer migrate great distances between their winter and summer homes. In summer, they head for the coast to feed on the lush vegetation and to escape swarms of biting flies. In winter, they hide in the forest to escape the worst of the weather.

Snow goose migration

Greater snow geese

Arctic

USA southern states

## Hibernating squirrels

The Arctic ground squirrel is mainly active in summer and lives where there is sandy soil, so it can dig a burrow. It feeds on tundra plants. In winter, it is one of the few Arctic animals to hibernate. During hibernation, the squirrel's body temperature drops to the lowest known of any mammal—its heart rate slows to one beat per minute, and, amazingly, it remains that way for up to eight months of the year.

## America's eagle

One Arctic predator is the American bald eagle. It has two layers of feathers that keep it warm, and its keen eyesight enables it to see its prey from over half a mile (more than 1 km) away. This means that a bald eagle flying as high as the clouds can search a huge area and pinpoint hares, fish, and squirrels to eat.

## Swift hares

The Arctic hare is active throughout the year. It has smaller ears and shorter legs than other hares to reduce heat loss, is able to store plenty of body fat, and has a thick coat of fur to keep it warm. To avoid the worst of the weather, the hare digs a hollow in the ground or in the snow. Many Arctic predators try to catch hares, but they have to be fast because the Arctic hare can run at 37 miles (60 km) per hour.

# PEOPLE OF THE ARCTIC

Despite the harshness of the climate and the remoteness of the Arctic, there are people who call it home. Of the many different groups, some have turned to the sea for their living, others to the land. Either way, it is a tough life in the cold and snow.

## Inuit nations

The Inuit of Alaska (Iñupiat), Canada (Inuvialuit), and Greenland (Kalaallit) are people of the frozen sea. They hunt whales, seals, and walrus, and they fish in the sea, lakes, and rivers. They travel by dog sled in winter and by boat in summer, and have a rich folklore, much of it relating to the nature around them. One story told to Inuit children says, "If you whistle at the aurora, the lights will come down and take you away or cut off your head."

## Saami people

The Saami people herding reindeer.

The Saami live in northern Scandinavia and northwest Russia, where they herd reindeer and sheep. In the mountains, they trap fur animals, and on the coast they catch fish. Some follow their reindeer herds north and south with the seasons. Reindeer provide them with meat, fur, and transport.

# The Arctic today

Nowadays, many people in the Arctic live in modern villages and towns and work in the oil, gas, and tourist industries. Some, though, still live in small settlements and live much as their ancestors did thousands of years ago.

Houses in Arctic villages are well-insulated to keep in the warmth.

# The visitors

The Arctic has become important for scientists studying climate change and Arctic wildlife, and for the military who set up facilities for spying, testing missiles, and building early warning systems to prevent missile attacks. Alert, at the north end of Ellesmere Island in Arctic Canada, is a Canadian Armed Forces base and weather station. It is the northernmost permanently-inhabited place in the world. Russia's most northerly military base is Nagurskoye, in the western part of Franz Josef Land.

The Nagurskoye air base

# INTREPID EXPLORATION

Humans have been fascinated with the Arctic for thousands of years. One of the first explorers was the ancient Greek sailor Pytheas. In 325BCE, he went north in search of tin, sailing from the Mediterranean to Cornwall and then even farther north. He described finding a "curdled sea," so he may well have reached the edge of the frozen Arctic Ocean.

## Northwest Passage

The Northwest Passage is a route from the Atlantic Ocean to the Pacific Ocean via the Arctic. The first European who tried to find a passage was Italian navigator John Cabot. In 1497 he tried and failed to discover a route through the ice. Many more attempts followed, but ships were crushed by the ice and their crews lost, like the ill-fated voyage of HMS *Terror* and HMS *Erebus*. It was not until 1906 that Norwegian explorer Roald Amundsen found a way through, but parts of the route were too shallow for trading ships. Today, however, with large-scale ice melts in summer, icebreaker cruise ships regularly pass through the Northwest Passage.

## Arctic challenge

During the 19th century, three goals dominated Arctic exploration: reaching the North Pole; finding a Northwest Passage; and discovering a Northeast Passage to the north of Europe and Asia. Opening these two trade routes was important to shorten the distance ships had to travel between the Atlantic and Pacific oceans.

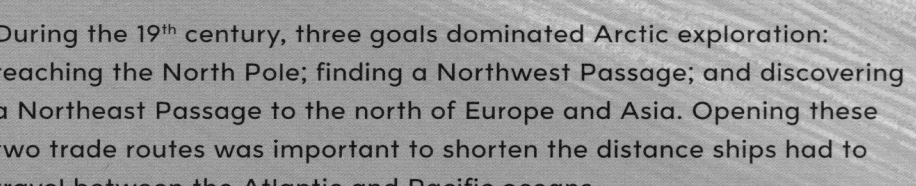

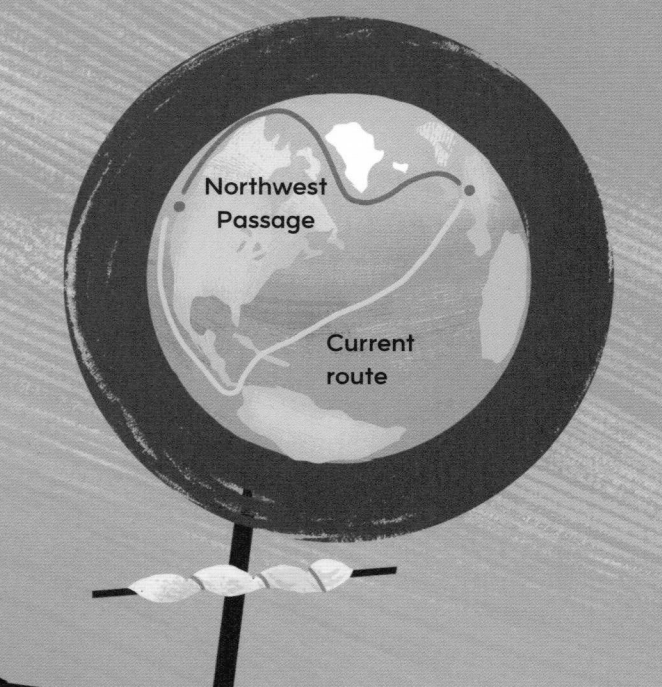

Northwest Passage

Current route

## Northeast Passage

This route also saw many failed attempts and the loss of ships and crews. It was not until 1878 that the Swedish-Finnish explorer Adolf Erik Nordenskiöld and the Vega Expedition became the first to find a Northeast Passage.

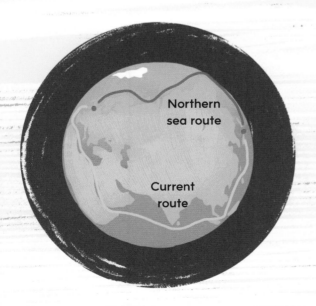

Northern sea route

Current route

## Race to the North Pole

Americans Frederick Cook and Robert Peary both claimed to have been the first to reach the Pole in 1908 and 1909 respectively, but both claims are questioned. The first person confirmed to have reached the North Pole was American Ralph Plaisted and his team in 1968, but they used snowmobiles. The first to travel on foot and dog sled was Wally Herbert in 1969. In 1995, the first to ski there, with no help at all, were Canadian Richard Weber and Russian Misha Malakhov.

The snowmobile is the workhorse of the Arctic—it's like a motorbike on skis.

# THE ARCTIC IN THE MODERN WORLD

Global warming caused by humans is melting more and more of the Arctic's sea ice. The result is that there is less thick ice than there used to be, and this is having disastrous consequences.

## Ice loss

Loss of thick sea ice means that walruses have fewer ice floes on which to rest, and polar bears must swim greater distances between ice floes in order to hunt seals. One bear fitted with a tracking device was found to have swum non-stop for a staggering 427 miles (687 km) over a period of nine days! Scientists believe its long and exhausting journey was the direct result of climate change.

## Lasting pollution

Hundreds of pollutants from industry are carried by winds to the Arctic. Here, they enter the food chain, where a single alga might absorb one molecule of pollutant, but a krill might eat 1,000 algae. So, one krill will have accumulated maybe 1,000 pollutant molecules. An Arctic cod eats 100 krill, a seal then eats several cod, and a polar bear eats several seals. At each stage the level of pollutant increases. Animals at the top of the food chain, such as polar bears, have the highest concentrations of pollutants. As a consequence, polar bear mothers are feeding their cubs contaminated milk, and this might affect whether a cub survives.

Arctic oil and natural gas exploration rig

The Trans-Alaska Pipeline System for oil stretches 800 miles (1,287 km) from Prudhoe Bay on the edge of the Arctic Ocean to Valdez in southern Alaska. Crossing points enable reindeer to follow traditional migration routes.

Reindeer

## Oil and natural gas

The Arctic has vast amounts of useful natural resources. The US Geological Survey estimates that nearly a quarter of the world's oil and natural gas lies beneath the Arctic. This poses a threat to the region: burning these fuels increases global warming, and a major oil spill at a drilling site could be devastating for Arctic wildlife.

# CONTENTS

# WHAT IS THE ANTARCTIC?

The Antarctic is the southernmost part of planet Earth. It includes the ice-covered Antarctic mainland, nearby islands, and the surrounding stormy Southern Ocean. Groups of rocky sub-Antarctic islands, such as South Georgia and the Aukland Islands, lie farther to the north.

## Ice sheet

An ice sheet more than 1.2 miles (2 km) thick covers almost all of the Antarctic mainland. In several places the ice pushes out over the sea, but does not break off, so an "ice shelf" is formed. The front of the ice shelf can tower about 200 feet (60 m) above the sea and stretch 500 miles (800 km) along the coast. Small icebergs break away constantly in a process called "calving," but every few years, truly massive icebergs break from the shelf. One of the largest in recent times was four times as big as Greater London!

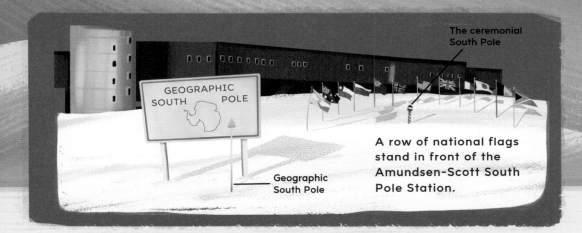

The ceremonial
South Pole

GEOGRAPHIC
SOUTH POLE

A row of national flags stand in front of the Amundsen-Scott South Pole Station.

Geographic
South Pole

Explorers
on the ice

Magnetic
North Pole

Geographic
North Pole

Geographic
South Pole

Magnetic
South Pole

## Three poles

The Earth spins around an imaginary line, like a spinning top. The southern point of this line is the "geographic" South Pole, but because the ice moves, the stick that marks the Pole has to be repositioned occasionally! Nearby is another pole—the "magnetic" South Pole. This is at the southern end of the Earth's magnetic field (an invisible area of force that surrounds our planet). Compass needles point toward the magnetic South Pole, but this pole moves too! When the Earth's magnetic field changes, the magnetic pole shifts its position. Nearby is a striped pole with a glass orb on top known as the "ceremonial" South Pole, which is used for photos.

# A bug's life

The Antarctic Peninsula is home to many of the Antarctic's land animal and plant residents. There are no polar bears here though—in fact, the largest land predator is a tiny reddish mite about 0.04 inch (1 mm) long, and the largest land animal is the flightless Antarctic midge which is no more than 0.24 inch (6 mm) long!

Rhagidia

Flightless Antarctic midge (Belgica antarctica)

Antarctic bugs

# Nunatak birds

Nunataks are large rocky outcrops that stick out above the ice sheet. Even though they can be hundreds of miles from the sea, seabirds such as snow petrels breed here. Apart from the nunataks, rocks are few and far between in many parts of the Antarctic mainland. These birds prefer to nest in rocky crevices to protect themselves from the weather and nest-raiding south polar skuas. They often fight for the best nest sites, spewing orange stomach oils at each other. If the gunk sticks, the bird is doomed because its feathers are no longer waterproof.

# MYSTERY LAKES AND ICE CHIMNEYS

The Western part of the Antarctic mainland has many volcanoes, most of them hidden below the ice sheet; in fact, the region has one of the highest concentrations of volcanoes in the world. At least one of the volcanoes under the ice is known to be active.

## The Antarctic's most active volcano

Mount Erebus on Ross Island is the mainland's most active volcano. It is one of the few volcanoes on Earth that has a lakeof hot molten rock or lava in its crater. The volcano erupts frequently, lobbing lava bombs at scientists climbing its slopes. Some of these flying blobs are as big as buses!

## Ancient lakes

Deep under the Antarctic ice sheet are more than 400 hidden lakes. At 155 miles (250 km) long and 30 miles (50 km) wide, Lake Vostock is the largest. Water samples sucked up through long, deep boreholes show that some lakes have been sealed off from the outside world for at least 15 million years.

Scientists exploring a Mount Erebus ice cave.

## Ice caves and chimneys

On the sides of Mount Erebus are strange openings in the ground, called "fumaroles." This is where hot steam and hot gases escape. The heat melts the underside of the ice and snow, creating large ice caves and tunnels. Inside, the temperature can be 43 degrees Fahrenheit (6°C), while it is -31 degrees Fahrenheit (-35°C) outside. As soon as escaping steam hits the cold air above, it freezes and builds up tall ice chimneys, some reaching as high as 59 feet (18 m).

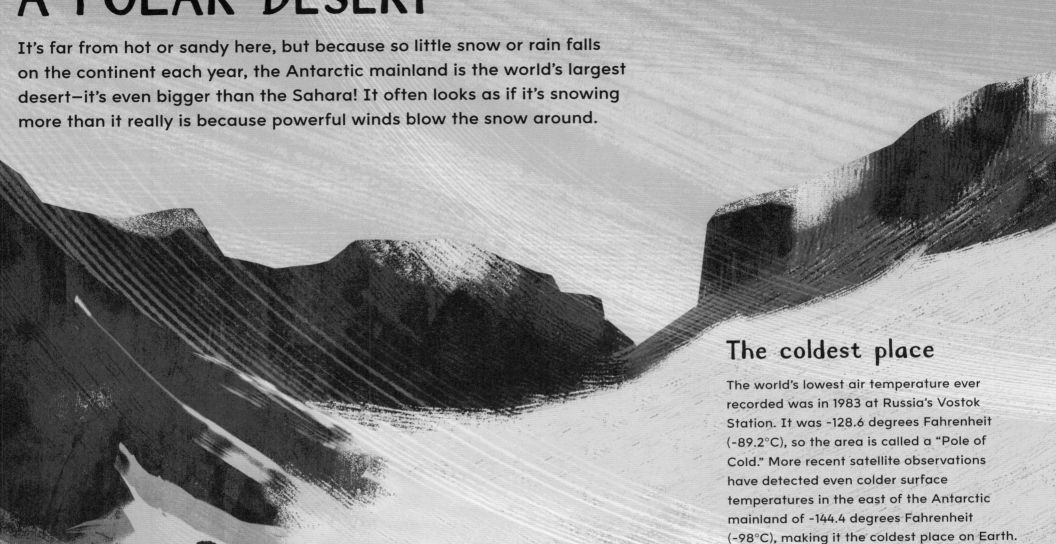

# A POLAR DESERT

It's far from hot or sandy here, but because so little snow or rain falls on the continent each year, the Antarctic mainland is the world's largest desert—it's even bigger than the Sahara! It often looks as if it's snowing more than it really is because powerful winds blow the snow around.

## The coldest place

The world's lowest air temperature ever recorded was in 1983 at Russia's Vostok Station. It was -128.6 degrees Fahrenheit (-89.2°C), so the area is called a "Pole of Cold." More recent satellite observations have detected even colder surface temperatures in the east of the Antarctic mainland of -144.4 degrees Fahrenheit (-98°C), making it the coldest place on Earth.

# Dry valleys

The McMurdo Dry Valleys are located in the Transantarctic Mountains, near McMurdo Sound. Instead of being buried in ice, they are mainly dry and barren. Amazingly, there is life here though. Bacteria that use sunlight to make their food live behind very thin slivers of rock that let the light through. The microbes grow in their own microscopic greenhouses.

# Lost seals

The strangest things to be found in these dry valleys are mummified seals; it's so dry and windy that the bodies do not decay normally. Some have been shown to be up to 2,500 years old, and how they came to be here is still a mystery. Scientists think they might be the remains of young seals that took a wrong turn on their way to the sea.

# Blood Falls

Blood-red water sometimes flows out from a salty lake under the Taylor Glacier. It falls into Lake Bonney, on the floor of a dry valley. Known as Blood Falls, the red color is from iron in the water that turns to rust.

# UNDERSEA GIANTS

Above the Antarctic ice there is very little color, but under the sea ice and ice shelves lies a multicolored world of marine invertebrates (animals without backbones). As well as a range of giant creatures, there are fragile featherstars that use their feathery arms to rise up from the seabed, and colorful starfish that cover the sea floor like a carpet.

## Below the ice

Among the creatures below the ice are giant isopods, similar to the woodlouse in your garden, but much bigger at 3.5 inches (9 cm) long. Sea spiders with tiny bodies but a leg span of up to 28 inches (70 cm) also lurk here. These giants grow slowly and live for an unusually long time.

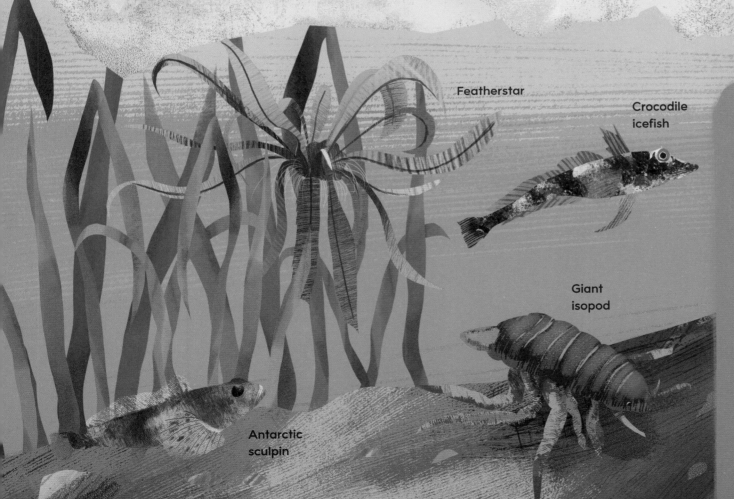

Featherstar

Crocodile icefish

Giant isopod

Antarctic sculpin

## Nightmare predators

The Antarctic scaleworm has a "golden fleece" of bristles around its body and a vicious snout that turns inside out to reveal large jaws with sharp teeth. Although only 8 inches (20 cm) long, this incredible predator can extend its jaws 2 inches (5 cm) in front of its body!

Antarctic scaleworm

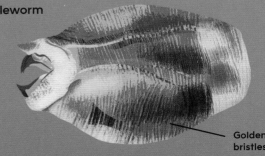

Golden bristles

## See-through icefish

Ghostly icefish, such as the crocodile icefish, live in Antarctic coastal waters. They have a sort of antifreeze in their blood to stop them from turning to ice. Cold water has high levels of oxygen dissolved in it, so icefish can absorb it through their skin as well as their gills. This means they don't need red blood cells to transport oxygen around their bodies like mammals do.

The "death star" is the nickname given to the terrifying starfish that is the size of a large dinner plate and has up to 50 long, slender arms. They use the tips of their upturned arms like fishing rods to grab passing krill and even small fish.

Giant sea spider

Starfish

"Death star" starfish

Nemertean worm

Krill

Sea urchin

"Basket" of modified legs for gathering food

Swimming legs

## Swarms of shrimp

The shrimp-like Antarctic krill is the most important food for animals in the Southern Ocean. In summer, swarms can be many miles across, making the sea look red. They are food for baleen whales, seals, fish, squid, penguins, and other seabirds.

# PENGUIN POWER

Penguins have stubby wings that act as flippers and enable them to "fly" underwater. They can dive deep and remain underwater for a long time. Backward-pointing barbs on their tongue prevent food such as slippery fish and squid from escaping, while tightly packed feathers and a thick layer of blubber keep the penguins warm.

## Emperor penguin

The world's largest penguin is the emperor. It has an unusual lifecycle and rears its chicks on the Antarctic ice during winter. The female lays a single egg and passes it to the male. He balances it on his feet, so it is not touching the ice, and a thick fold of skin covers the egg to protect it from the cold. The female, meanwhile, heads to sea to feed. The male then incubates the egg (keeps it warm) and later cares for the chick. To conserve heat, many males huddle together. When the female returns and takes over babysitting duties, the male goes to sea. In the summer months, when the weather and food are better, the youngster is ready to face the world alone.

## Deepest divers

Emperor penguins dive the deepest of any seabird while hunting for fish and squid. They can be down for up to 22 minutes, at depths of 330 to 660 feet (100 to 200 m), but they can go deeper. One daring penguin was tracked to a depth of 1,854 feet (565 m)!

# Adélie penguin

The Adélie builds a pebble nest so, if the snow all around it melts, the nest on its mound is not flooded. Pebbles are often in short supply though, so penguins tend to steal from each other.

# Gentoo penguin

When gentoo chicks are bigger, they beg for food from any penguin. This means penguin parents have to race around the colony to make sure they are feeding their own chicks, all the while listening for their baby's unique call.

# Chinstrap penguin

The chinstrap brings back about 10.5 ounces (300 g)of krill for its two chicks on each fishing trip. When the young can keep themselves warm, they gather in crèches for safekeeping. This means both parents can be away from the nest at the same time.

14

# THE SEAL DEAL

Antarctic seals spend much of their time under the sea ice catching fish, squid, or krill. In the water, they are graceful, but on land they are lumbering creatures. The seals clamber on top of the ice to rest or give birth.

## Crabeater seal

Crabeaters spend all their life in pack ice and on ice floes (floating slabs of ice). Despite their name, they do not eat crabs; instead, they have special teeth that enable them to filter krill from the seawater.

## Weddell seal

Weddell seals prefer to stay on ice that is attached to the land and does not move. They hunt under the ice for up to 45 minutes, before coming up for air. They make several breathing holes in the ice, which they cleverly keep open using their teeth.

# Ross seal

Ross seals have small mouths and needle-sharp teeth to catch slippery fish and squid. They have large eyes, and are thought to hunt in the dark depths of the Southern Ocean.

# Leopard seal

This seal has a large lizard-like head and powerful jaws lined with sharp teeth. Leopard seals eat penguins and young seals, but their teeth are similar to crabeaters', so they can also filter out krill. They will also eat fish and squid.

# ULTIMATE POLAR PREDATOR

The orca, or killer whale, is the top (apex) predator, both in the Antarctic and the Arctic. It is the largest member of the dolphin family, with males growing up to 26 feet (8 m) long. Orcas have powerful jaws and rows of sharp, cone-shaped teeth for grabbing anything from fish to seals and other whales. They can see well below and above the water, and they push their heads above the surface—called "spyhopping"—to check for prey.

## Orca types

Orcas travel in family groups known as pods, and they all hunt together. Scientists have found that there are at least four different kinds of Antarctic orcas, with each group specializing in catching a particular type of prey.

## Whale hunters

Type A orcas gang up on minke whales, the smallest type of baleen whale. They swim around the whale, attacking from the sides and swimming below and on top to try to stop it from taking a breath. The minke whale eventually becomes exhausted and is easy to catch.

## Seal hunters

Type B orcas catch seals. To do so, they have developed a remarkably successful hunting technique. The whales line up alongside each other and then swim directly at a seal resting on an ice floe. Together, they create a huge wave that washes the seal into the water, which gives them a better chance to catch it.

## Fish hunters

Type C and D orcas focus on fish, with type C catching Antarctic toothfish among the ice floes and type D orcas catching the Patagonian toothfish away from the ice.

# SUMMER VISITORS

Baleen whales were hunted a lot by humans during the 19th and 20th centuries. An international ban on whaling has allowed whale populations to recover. Now, large numbers of whales make journeys to the Antarctic each summer to feed on the great quantity of food available at this time of year, especially krill.

## Minke whale

The Antarctic minke whale is one of the smallest species of baleen whale. It is up to 36 feet (11 m) long and its small size meant it was mostly ignored by whalers. Today, it is the most common whale in the Antarctic.

Humpback whales

## Humpback whale

The humpback has a particularly clever way to round up its food, called bubble-net fishing. One or two whales dive below a swarm of krill, and then spiral up to the surface blowing bubbles all the time. This frightens the krill into the middle of the rising cylinder of bubbles, where they are trapped. The whales then rise up, open their mouths, and grab as many krill as they can. Up at the surface, the whales look like giant flowers opening.

**Humpback whales bubble-net fishing**

Bubbles of
air made by
the whales

## Blue whale

This, the largest animal that has ever lived,
is just a summer visitor to the Antarctic.
Blue whales can grow up to 108 feet (33 m)
long. When feeding, the blue whale takes a
huge mouthful of seawater and krill, then,
using its enormous tongue, it pushes the water
out through its comblike baleen plates. A great
ball of krill is left behind, and then swallowed
in one gigantic gulp!

## Fin whale

The second largest whale is the fin whale. Recently great numbers of
fin whales—possibly the largest number of giant whales ever seen feeding
in one place—have been spotted catching krill in the Drake Passage. This is
an area in the Southern Ocean, between the southern tip of South America and
the Antarctic Peninsula, which is prone to violent storms.

# BATTLES IN THE DEEP

Two of nature's giants hunt in Antarctic waters—the sperm whale and the colossal squid. The squid hunts fish and other squid, and the whale hunts colossal squid. When caught, the squid puts up a huge fight. Large round scars found on sperm whales' heads show just how brutal the battles can be. The scars are from the rows of swiveling hooks and sharp teeth that line the edge of the suckers on the squid's tentacles. There are also rows of hooks and suckers on its eight arms.

## Sperm whale

Sperm whales visiting the Antarctic are all males. They have large cone-shaped teeth in their lower jaw, useful for gripping slippery squid and fish, which are slurped down whole. The huge forehead is filled with waxy oil, which was highly prized by whalers.

## Echolocation

Sperm whales find their way in the darkness of the deep sea using sounds, a skill known as echolocation. The whales emit very loud, high frequency clicks which bounce off any object ahead. The returning echoes give the whale information about the object: whether it is living, which way it is moving, and how big it is.

## Colossal squid

As its name suggests, this species of squid is the largest
known invertebrate. From the end of its body to the tip of its
tentacles, it can measure 46 feet (14 m). The colossal squid also
has the world's biggest eyes—they are the size of soccer balls!
Little is known about the squid or its behavior because very
few have ever been seen.

# ANTARCTIC'S FLYING BIRDS

The Antarctic is famous for its penguins, but there are also many species of flying birds living and nesting on the mainland and nearby islands. Some arrive for the summer to breed, while others live in the Antarctic all year round.

## Snowy sheathbill

The snowy sheathbill is not a seabird and finds most of its food on the land. Not at all fussy and rather ruthless, it eats almost anything that is edible. It steals regurgitated fish and krill from penguins feeding their chicks. It will take eggs and even kill chicks. It also scavenges on dead bodies, will go through the trash bins at Antarctic research bases, and eats seal poop!

## Southern giant petrel

Male southern giant petrels scavenge meat from dead carcasses and often squabble with other birds, holding out their wings to keep all the food for themselves. Females, however, tend to eat live prey, such as krill, fish, and squid.

## A tern with two summers

Antarctic terns live in the Antarctic, but it might come as a surprise to learn that *Arctic* terns live here too. Arctic terns nest in the Arctic during the northern summer, and fly to feeding sites in the Antarctic during the southern summer. A typical return journey between the Arctic and the Antarctic is about 44,000 miles (70,800 km). One tern flew even farther—an amazing 60,000 miles (96,000 km)—the longest known migration of any animal.

Arctic tern migration route

Arctic

Antarctic

# Antarctic shag

The shag is an expert diver. It chases and catches fish and shellfish underwater, often hunting together with other shags; in fact, in winter these birds gather in large flocks. Hundreds of birds form dense rafts in the ocean. Antarctic shags have bright blue eyes and a beige-colored growth on the top of their bill.

Antarctic terns

# ANTARCTIC EXPLORATION

Since people first began to explore the world, the prospect of an icy continent at the bottom of the Earth was often talked about. In 350 $_{BCE}$, the ancient Greeks were first to suggest it. They knew the Arctic existed, and thought there should be another cold area at the other end of the planet to balance things out.

## First to arrive

English navigator James Cook was first to cross the Antarctic Circle and sail around the entire continent in 1773, but solid sea ice prevented him from getting close enough to actually see the land. The first to see land was Russian naval officer Captain Thaddeus Bellingshausen, in January 1820. The first landing was by American sealer John Davis on February 7, 1821.

## First at the Pole

The race to reach the South Pole first was a close one. British explorer Sir Robert Falcon Scott was just beaten to it by Norwegian explorer Roald Amundsen on December 14, 1911. Scott reached the Pole 35 days later only to find Amundsen's tent and flag standing there. Scott's team did not survive the return journey.

## South Pole crossings

The first successful crossing of the whole Antarctic mainland, via the South Pole, was by British geologist Vivian Fuchs and New Zealand mountaineer Edmund Hillary. They traveled in Sno-Cats (caterpillar-tracked vehicles). In 1997, Norwegian explorer Børge Ousland became the first person to cross the continent unsupported. He went on skis and pulled a sled, using the wind and a kite to whiz along on the flat parts.

## Scott's hut

There are two huts in the Antarctic that were built by Robert Falcon Scott and his team. The hut built in 1911 at Cape Evans is now preserved as a historic monument. It was from this wooden hut that Scott and his colleagues set out to reach the Pole on their ill-fated expedition.

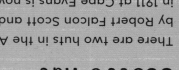

# PEOPLE OF THE ANTARCTIC

Nobody lives permanently in the Antarctic—everybody is a visitor, and usually working at a research station. There are about 45 stations that operate all year, and another 30 summer stations. Scientists study problems such as climate change. A summer temperature of 64.9 degrees Fahrenheit (18.3°C) was recorded in 2020, near the northern tip of the Antarctic Peninsula —the highest temperature ever recorded on the Antarctic continent.

## Antarctic treaty

The Antarctic treaty is an agreement that sets aside the Antarctic mainland as a scientific preserve, and includes a ban on any military activity and mining for minerals. As of 2019, 54 nations have signed the treaty.

**McMURDO STATION ANTARCTICA**

## Antarctic's largest base

USA's McMurdo Station is the largest research station. It has 100 buildings, the world's southernmost harbor, three airfields, and a heliport, and is located at the southern tip of Ross Island in McMurdo Sound. It even has its own golf course!

# Ivan the Terra Bus

Due to the nature of the terrain, with ice and snow dominating for much of the year, research station workers get around on all sorts of strange vehicles. One of the main workhorses is the Sno-Cat. It is like a tractor, but with caterpillar tracks on the front and rear. Another is the Hägglunds, a box-shaped cabin on caterpillar tracks. At McMurdo Station people get around on Ivan the Terra Bus, a bus with super-sized tires.

# Mobile base

UK's Halley VI Research Station is unusual. It has hydraulic legs fitted with skis, so it can be moved. It is the first research station capable of doing this. Halley's eight living and working modules are built on a floating ice shelf in the Weddell Sea. If cracks appear in the ice nearby, the base can be moved quickly.

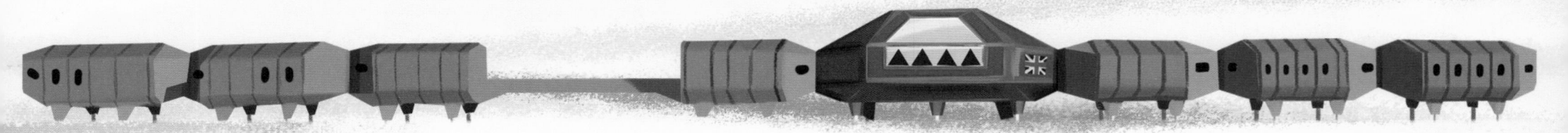

# ISLAND LIFE

Where the Southern Ocean meets the southernmost parts of the Atlantic, Pacific, and Indian oceans, there are sub-Antarctic islands. Parts of these islands are generally ice-free, but they are battered by strong winds all year. Despite this, they are packed with wildlife, especially in summer. It's the perfect time to breed because the sea is filled with plenty of food for growing babies.

## Dangerous winds

The Southern Ocean is one of the windiest places on Earth and this can be a problem for albatrosses. Chicks of the gray-headed albatross sit on a nest that looks like a tall cushion. Sometimes, the wind blows them out of the nest. If they cannot get back in again, they are doomed, because the parents will only feed a chick that is inside the nest—even if a chick is sitting right beside the nest, sadly it goes hungry.

## Wandering albatross

Several types of albatrosses breed on sub-Antarctic islands. The wandering albatross has the longest wingspan of any bird, up to 11.5 feet (3.5 m). It can glide over the wave tops, using air currents pushed up by the waves, to travel great distances in search of food, such as squid and fish.

## King penguin

The king penguin is another penguin with an unusual life cycle. It can take 13 months from the time the egg is laid to the time the chick leaves its parents. At six weeks old, chicks have thick downy coats. Because of this, in the 19th century people thought these chicks were actually a separate species. They gather together in crèches while their parents are at sea.

In winter, large chicks may wait between four and six weeks for parents to return with food.

# Elephant seal

The world's largest type of seal is the southern elephant seal. Males can be 19 feet (5.8 m) long and weigh as much as a small car, but females are considerably smaller. In early spring, the seals haul out on beaches on sub-Antarctic islands, such as South Georgia, where large males battle for the right to be "beachmaster." When at sea, these seals can dive down to 7,835 feet (2,388 m) for up to 120 minutes while hunting fish and squid.

# BACK FROM THE BRINK

During the 19th and 20th centuries, sealers and whalers not only killed whales, but also enormous numbers of seals, sea lions, fur seals, and penguins in the Antarctic and sub-Antarctic. They were after their fur and oil for the lamps that lit people's homes. Many species were hunted almost to extinction, but since the ban on hunting, thankfully populations have increased again.

## Antarctic fur seal

Fur seals were killed in huge numbers, but they have been protected since the early 20th century. Recovery is not the same everywhere however as some seals become entangled in fishing gear or pieces of plastic, and others struggle to find enough food. Nevertheless, fur seal populations have grown enormously. On South Georgia, where the majority of Atlantic fur seals live, there are about seven million fur seals. Good news for a change!

## New Zealand sea lion

Like the whales, these sea lions were hunted to near extinction, and they are not free of threats even today. Diseases kill pups, and adults are caught in fishing nets. The sea around the Auckland Islands, which is home to a large population, has been declared a marine reserve, so many sea lions are now protected.

New Zealand sea lion

## Southern right whale

This whale was the "right" whale to catch; it was inquisitive, so it approached whaling ships rather than fleeing them, and when harpooned it floated. Numbers plummeted, so a hunting ban was introduced in 1937. Now, slowly, the whales are returning to sub-Antarctic islands, like the Auckland Islands, where they traditionally gathered to breed.